My Granny's a Juggler

Written by Simone-Louise Lalande
Illustrated by Jan van der Voo

When my granny came
to babysit,
she didn't cook
and she didn't knit.

She got dressed up
in her juggler's clothes,
and pressed on her face
a big red nose.

3

She threw a banana in the air,
with two red apples
and one green pear.

And do you think
she let them fall?

No! No! No!
Not at all!

She balanced a houseplant
on her head,
and tossed in the air
a loaf of bread.

And do you think
she let them fall?

No! No! No!
Not at all!

She twitched her nose
and winked an eye,
then scooped up my doll
and a blackberry pie.

And do you think
she let them fall?

No! No! No!
Not at all!

9

She ran up the stairs
and slid down with a hoot,
and threw in the air
an old rubber boot.

And do you think
she let them fall?

No! No! No!
Not at all!

She grabbed two pineapples,
tossed them up,
and then she grabbed
my favorite cup.

And do you think
she let them fall?

No! No! No!
Not at all!

13

She put our cat
on one of her knees,
and flung up my teddy
as quick as a sneeze.

And do you think
she let them fall?

No! No! No!
Not at all!

14

She tossed up a bowl
full of water and fish,
then reached for a teapot
and Mom's special dish.

And do you think
she let them fall?

No! No! No!
Not at all!

She did a quick jig
and jumped on a chair,
and then threw a dozen
brown eggs in the air.

And do you think
she let them fall?

No! No! No!
Not at all!

18

Oh no! My dog knocked
over the chair,
and my juggling granny
went through the air,
   and
      the . . .
fruit and the bread,
and the plant on her head,

20

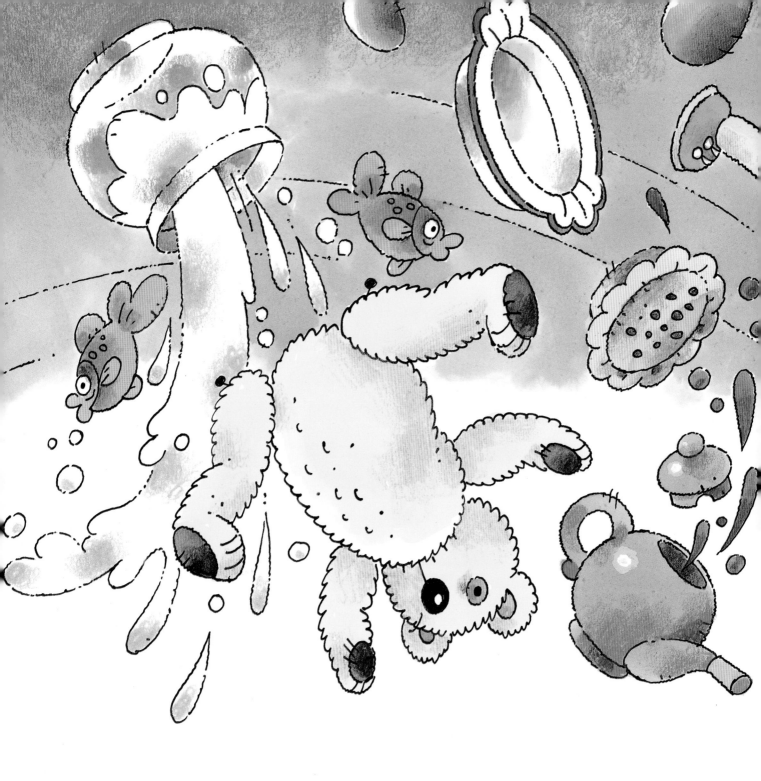

and the teapot and dish,
and the bowl full of fish,
my bear with one eye,
and the big yummy pie,

22

and my favorite cup too,
and the eggs really flew,
and the doll with the hat,
and our big pussy cat . . . .

Do you think Granny
let them fall?

CRASH! BANG!
She dropped them all!

24